All about Olivia Rodrigo

INCLUDES FACTS, INSPIRING QUOTES, QUIZZES, ACTIVITIES AND MUCH, MUCH MORE.

ISBN: 978-1-83990-419-6

LULU AND BELL: 2024

This book is an unofficial book and is not authorized, sponsored or endorsed by Olivia Rodrigo.

Fact File

OLIVIA RODRIGO

From: California

Zodiac Sign: Pisces

DOB: 20th February 2003

Height: 5ft 4inches

Siblings: none

Olivia's father is of Filipino descent while her mother has German and Irish ancestry.

FUN FACTS:

1. Her middle name is Isabel.

2. She was born half-deaf in her left ear.

3. She attended Lisa J. Mails Elementary School.

FAVORITE COLORS:

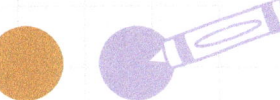

FUN FACTS:

1. Her first main role was acting in the Disney series "Bizaardvark."

2. Olivia played the character Paige.

3. Olivia appeared in High School Musical: The Musical: The Series.

4. She played the character Nini Salazar-Roberts.

She moved to Los Angeles when she got the part in Bizaardvark and was home-schooled.

She wrote 'All I Want' the song from High School Musical: The Musical: The Series, sang by her character.

She left the series after season three.

I LOVE SONGS WHERE YOU CAN LISTEN TO THEM AND SORT OF FEEL LIKE YOU'RE IN ANOTHER WORLD... AND THE WAY YOU DO THAT IS THROUGH IMAGERY AND DETAILS.

OLIVIA RODRIGO

She could play the guitar by the age of 12.

FUN FACTS:

1. She signed with Geffen Records in 2020.

2. She released her debut single in 2021 it was called 'drivers Licence.'

3. 'Drivers License' debuted at number one on Billboard Hot 100.

She grew up listening to alternative rock music including No Doubt, Pearl Jam and Green Day.

Olivia includes Taylor Swift and Lorde as her main Musical inspirations.

She called The White Stripes band member Jack White her 'hero of all heroes.'

SHE WROTE AGED 17

drivers license

At 18 she became the youngest artist to debut at number one on the Billboard Hot 100 Chart.

FUN FACTS:

1. Drivers License became one of the best-selling songs of 2021.

2. Her follow-up single "Deja Vu" debuted at number eight on the Billboard Hot 100 making her the first artist to debut their first two releases in the top 10 of the Hot 100.

Olivia's first album was called 'Sour.'

FROM A YOUNG AGE, I REALIZED THAT VULNERABILITY EQUATES TO STRENGTH AND THAT'S SO TRUE IN MY SONGWRITING.

OLIVIA RODRIGO

In 2021 she premiered a prom-themed concert film on YouTube called Sour Prom.

She was named Entertainer of the Year in 2021 by Time magazine.

FUN FACTS:

1. Olivia is a huge Twilight fan.

2. She was a big One Direction fan.

3. Her mother is normally the first to hear her new songs.

She received "Songwriter of the Year" honors in 2021 by Variety.

"I THINK SHOWING UP IS REALLY IMPORTANT. IT'S MORE IMPOTANT THAN BEING TALENTED OR GOOD AT ANYTHING BECAUSE YOU CAN BE SUPER TALENTED, BUT IF YOU DON'T SHOW UP, WHAT'S THE POINT?"

OLIVIA RODRIGO

In 2022 a documentary was released on Disney called Olivia Rodrigo:Driving Home 2 U.

FUN FACTS:

1. In 2023 she released her second album called Guts.

2. The Single Vampire was released in June 2023 and topped the Billboard Hot 100

Purple is her favourite colour, she says it represents all things magical.

Olivia is a big vintage shopper.

I never want to stop learning and growing as a person.

OLIVIA RODRIGO

FAVOURITE OLIVIA RODRIGO SONGS

- Vampire
- Bad Idia right
- Pretty isnt Pretty
- Brutal
- Lacy
- Good 4 U
- 1 step forward 3 steps back

THIS OR THAT

- DEJA VU **OR** GOOD 4 U
- DRIVERS LICENSE **OR** VAMPIRE
- BAD IDEA RIGHT? **OR** GET HIM BACK!
- HAPPIER **OR** BRUTAL
- ALL I WANT **OR** CAN'T CATCH ME NOW
- GUTS **OR** SOUR
- FAVORITE CRIME **OR** JEALOUSY, JEALOUSY

HOW WELL DO YOU KNOW OLIVIA RODRIGO?

What is her favourite colour?

A) Purple

B) Blue

C) Green

D) Pink

HOW WELL DO YOU KNOW OLIVIA RODRIGO?

What is the name of the character she played in Bizaardvark?

A) Nini

B) Summer

C) Paige

D) Olivia

HOW WELL DO YOU KNOW OLIVIA RODRIGO?

What is her middle name?

A) Isabella

B) Isabel

C) Bella

D) India

HOW WELL DO YOU KNOW OLIVIA RODRIGO?

How old was she when she wrote drivers license?

A) 14

B) 16

C) 17

D) 18

HOW WELL DO YOU KNOW OLIVIA RODRIGO?

Her 2021 prom-themed concert film on YouTube was called?

A) Sour Party

B) Sour Prom

C) Olivia's Prom

D) Prom Party

HOW WELL DO YOU KNOW OLIVIA RODRIGO?

Answers

A) Purple

C) Paige

B) Isabel

C) 17

B) Sour Prom

My Top 5 Songs

Sour (2021)

GUTS (2023)

COMPLETE THE LYRICS

Red lights, stop signs
I still see your face in the _____

Show her off like she's a new _____

I've lost my mind, I've spent the night
Cryin' on the floor of my
_____

Play her piano, but she doesn't know
That I was the one who taught you
_____

And I hear your voice every time that I think
I'm not
_____

Favourite Olivia Rodrigo Song Lyrics

Favourite Olivia Rodrigo Song Lyrics

Favourite Olivia Rodrigo Song Lyrics

TOP OLIVIA RODRIGO SONG

FIRST SONG YOU HEARD

Gud 4 u

FAVOURITE SONG

Happier or Vampier

FAVOURITE LIVE SONG

FAVOURITE OLD SONG

Lacy? is that old

TOP OLIVIA RODRIGO SONGS

SONG YOU WOULD RECOMMEND TO A FRIEND

Gud 4 u

FAVOURITE NEW SONG

Vampeir

FAVOURITE ALBUM

Guts

SONG TO MAKE YOU FEEL HAPPY

happeir

CREATE YOUR OLIVIA RODRIGO FASHION INSPIRED LOOK

Olivia Rodrigo

— T-shirt
— backwards cap
— socks
— shoes
— denim jeans

CREATE YOUR OLIVIA RODRIGO FASHION INSPIRED LOOK

WRITE A SONG ABOUT...

- favourite season
- a lullaby
- your ideal day
- your ideal future
- things that make you happy
- things that make you sad
- being brave
- summer fun

NOTES

NOTES

NOTES

NOTES

NOTES

NOTES

NOTES

NOTES

NOTES